Y0-BRB-143

Other giftbooks by Exley:
A Portfolio of Business Jokes   A Knockout of Sports Jokes
Tennis Quotations   Golf Quotations

Published simultaneously in 1997 by Exley Publications in Great Britain and
Exley Giftbooks in the USA.

Copyright © Helen Exley 1997

12 11 10 9 8 7 6 5 4 3 2 1

ISBN 1-85015-807-X
A copy of the CIP data is available from the British Library on request. All
rights reserved. No part of this publication may be reproduced or transmitted
in any form or by any means, electronic or mechanical, including photocopy,
recording or any information storage and retrieval system without
permission in writing from the publisher.

Series Editor: Helen Exley.
Pictures selected by Helen Exley.
Text research by Judy Fireman.
Edited by Claire Lipscomb.
Pictures researched by Image Select, London.
Designed by Pinpoint Design Company.
Typeset by Delta, Watford.
Printed and bound in China.

Exley Publications Ltd, 16 Chalk Hill, Watford, Herts WD1 4BN, UK.
Exley Giftbooks, 232 Madison Avenue, Suite 1206, NY 10016, USA.

Acknowledgements: The publishers are grateful for permission to reproduce copyright
material. Whilst every effort has been made to trace copyright holders, the publishers would
be pleased to hear from any not here acknowledged. THOMAS BOSWELL: Extracts from *How
Life Imitates the World Series: An Inquiry into the Game* and the *Washington Post*, copyright ©
1982, 1991 by The Washington Post's Writers Group. Reprinted by permission of Doubleday
& Co., Inc. OGDEN NASH: "An Ump's Heart", copyright © 1966 Ogden Nash. Copyright
renewed 1975 by Frances Nash, Isabel Nash Eberstadt and Linnel Nash Smith. Reprinted by
permission of Little Brown & Co. Ltd, Boston and Curtis Brown Ltd, NY.
Picture credits: Exley Publications is very grateful to the following individuals and
organizations for permission to reproduce their pictures: Archiv fur Kunst (AKG), Art
Resource (AR), Artworks (AW), The Bridgeman Art Library (BAL), The Image Bank (TIB),
Superstock (SS): Cover: © 1997 Michael Dudash, *Man Sliding Into Home Plate*, TIB; title page:
© 1997 Todd Doney, *"Winding Up" To Throw*, TIB; p7: © 1997 Jane Wooster Scott, *Baseball
Game*, SS; p8: © 1997 Dan Brown, AW; p10/11: *Baseball-The American National Game*, AKG;
p12: © 1997 Morris Kantor, *Baseball at Night*, AR/BAL; p14/15: © 1997 Bart Forbes; p16: *Early
Baseball Game, New York*, TIB; p18: © 1997 Lance Richbourg, *Bat Boys*, SS; p20/21: © 1997
Stephane Poulin, *To The Glory of God*, BAL; p23: © 1997 Lance Richbourg, *"Goose" Goslin*, SS;
p24: © 1997 Liberty Collection, *Baseball Argument, Catcher and Umpire*, TIB; p27: © 1997
Lance Richbourg, *The Catch*, SS; p29: © 1997 Dan Brown, AW; p30/31: © 1997 Peter Fiore, AW; p30/31:
© 1997 Lance Richbourg, *The Run*, SS; p33: © 1997 Dan Brown, AW; p34: © 1997 Lance
Richbourg, *The Hit*, SS; p37: © 1997 Dan Brown, AW; p38/39: © 1997 Peter Fiore, AW; p41: ©
1997 Lance Richbourg, *First Out of a Double Play*, SS; p42: *Baseball Batter*, TIB; p45: © 1997
Bart Forbes; p46: © 1997 Lance Richbourg, *Sliding in Yankee Stadium*, SS; p48: © 1997 Rick
McCollum, TIB; p51: © 1997 Peter Fiore, AW; p53: © 1997 Bart Forbes; p54/55: © 1997 Dan
Brown, AW; p56/57: © 1997 Bart Forbes, TIB; p58/59: © 1997 Lance Richbourg, *The Polo
Grounds*, SS; p60/61: © 1997 Todd Doney, *Baseball Player Sliding Into Home*, TIB.

Baseball
QUOTATIONS
A COLLECTION OF STYLISH PICTURES
AND THE BEST BASEBALL QUOTES

EXLEY
NEW YORK • WATFORD, UK

THE GREAT AMERICAN GAME...

"Well – it's our game; that's the chief fact in connection with it: America's game; it has the snap, go, fling of the American atmosphere; it belongs as much to our institutions, fits into them as significantly as our Constitution's laws; is just as important in the sum total of our historic life."

WALT WHITMAN

●

"To be an American and unable to play baseball is comparable to being a Polynesian and unable to swim. It's an impossible situation."

JOHN CHEEVER
from "The National Pastime"

●

"Whoever wants to know the heart and mind of America had better learn baseball."

JACQUES BARZUN
from "God's Country and Mine"

"Baseball, because of its continuity over the space of America and the time of America, is a place where memory gathers."

DONALD HALL

"The game of baseball has always been linked in my mind with the mystic texture of childhood, with the sounds and smells of summer nights and with the memories of my father."

DORIS KEARNS GOODWIN
from "From Father, With Love" in the "Boston Globe", October 6, 1986

"It is by baseball, and not by other American sports, that our memories bronze themselves. Other sports change too fast, rise with the highrise, mutate for mutability, modify to modernize. By baseball we join hands with the long line of forefathers and with the dead."

DONALD HALL
from "Fathers Playing Catch with Sons: Essays on Sport (Mostly Baseball)"

"Is there anything that can evoke spring...
better than the sound of the ball smacking
into the pocket of the big mitt, the sound of
the bat as it hits the horsehide; for me...

almost everything I know about spring is
in it – the first leaf, the jonquil, the maple
tree, the smell of grass upon your hands and
knees, the coming into flower of April."

THOMAS WOLFE

CLEAN LINES AND CLEAR DECISIONS

"I think a baseball field must be the
most beautiful thing in the world. It's so
honest and precise."

LOWELL COHN
from "The Temple of Baseball"

"No game in the world is as tidy and
dramatically neat as baseball, with cause and
effect, crime and punishment, motive and
result, so cleanly defined."

PAUL GALLICO
Sportswriter

"Baseball is all clean lines and clear
decisions... wouldn't life be far easier if it
consisted of a series of definitive calls; safe or
out, fair or foul, strike or ball. Oh, for a
life like that...."

ERIC ROLFE GREENBERG
from "The Celebrant"

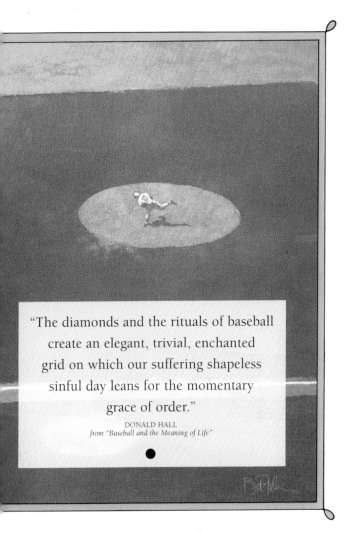

"The diamonds and the rituals of baseball
create an elegant, trivial, enchanted
grid on which our suffering shapeless
sinful day leans for the momentary
grace of order."

DONALD HALL
from "Baseball and the Meaning of Life"

FOR CONNOISSEURS ONLY

"Baseball fans love numbers. They love to swirl them around their mouths like Bordeaux wine."

PAT CONROY
Novelist

●

"Baseball is made up of very few big and dramatic moments, but rather it's a beautifully put together pattern of countless little subtleties that finally add up to the big moment, and you have to be well-versed in the game to truly appreciate them."

PAUL RICHARDS
Orioles manager 1955-1961

●

"Baseball is like church. Many attend, but few understand."

WES WESTRUM
Mets manager 1965-1967

●

"Baseball is for every boy a good, wholesome sport. It brings him out of the close confinement of the schoolroom. It takes the stoop from his shoulders and puts hard, honest muscle all over his frame. It rests his eyes, strengthens his lungs, and teaches him self-reliance and courage. Every mother ought to rejoice when her boy says he is on the school or college nine."

WALTER CAMP

●

"Baseball gives every American boy a chance to excel. Not just to be as good as someone else, but to be better. This is the nature of man and the name of the game."

TED WILLIAMS
Boston Red Sox outfielder 1939-1942, 1946-1960

●

"Baseball is green and safe.
It has neither the street
intimidation of basketball nor the controlled
Armageddon of football.... Baseball is a green
dream that happens on summer nights in
safe places in unsafe cities."

LUKE SALISBURY
from "The Answer is Baseball"

"Ever since the first caveman picked up the first cudgel, went to his front door and smacked the first nosy saber-toothed tiger in the snout, mankind has known the atavistic power and pleasure of the bat....
Now, that ancient inherited desire for thudding force, for an instrument that will deliver a satisfying blow, has descended to the baseball bat."

THOMAS BOSWELL
from "How Life Imitates the World Series"

●

"The pitcher has got only a ball. I've got a bat. So the percentage in weapons is in my favor and I let the fellow with the ball do the fretting."

HANK AARON
*Milwaukee & Atlanta Braves/Milwaukee Brewers 1954-1976,
quoted in the "Milwaukee Journal", July 31, 1956*

●

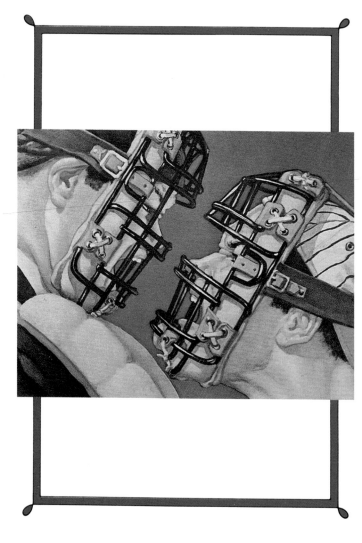

VIOLENCE UNDER WRAPS

"Baseball is a game, yes. It is also business.
But what it most truly is is disguised combat.
For all its gentility, its almost leisurely pace,
baseball is violence under wraps."

WILLY MAYS
New York Giants outfielder 1951-1972

●

"Sportsmanship and easygoing methods are
all right, but it is the prospect of a hot fight
that brings out the crowds."

JOHN McGRAW
New York Giants manager 1902-1932

●

"Baseball reflects American society's need
for confrontation."

W. J. WEATHERBY
in the "Manchester Guardian", 1988

●

"One of the chief duties of the fan is to engage in arguments with the man behind him. This department has been allowed to run down fearfully."

ROBERT BENCHLEY

●

"The true fan is not only violently partisan, but very noisy.... I used to amuse myself with wondering what would happen if a group of fans of this order would turn up at a tennis match or a golf meet."

W. R. BURNETT
Author

●

"I sat in the reserved seats and felt uncomfortable. Everybody is so polite... in the bleachers, however, you can be vindictive. Nearly everybody is."

ARNOLD HANO
from "A Day in the Bleachers"

●

THE MANAGER'S LOT

"Well, there are three things that
the average man thinks he can do better
than anybody else.
Build a fire, run a hotel and manage
a baseball team."

ROCKY BRIDGES

●

"The secret of managing is to keep
the guys who hate you away from the guys
who are undecided."

CASEY STENGEL
New York Yankees manager 1949-1960

●

"The toughest thing about managing is
standing up for nine innings."

PAUL OWENS
Philadelphia Phillies manager 1972, 1983-1984

●

"I like to look down on a field of
green and white, a summertime land of Oz,
a place to dream. I've never been unhappy
in a ballpark."

JIM MURRAY
in the "Los Angeles Times", 1986

●

"I believe in the church of baseball.
I've tried all the major religions and most of
the minor ones....
I know things. For instance, there are 108
beads in a Catholic's rosary and there are 108
stitches in a baseball. When I learned that, I
gave Jesus a chance. But it just didn't work
out between us. The Lord laid too much guilt
on me.... You see, there's no guilt in baseball.
And it's never boring.... It's a long season and
you gotta trust it. I've tried 'em all, I really
have, and the only church that truly feeds the
soul, day in, day out, is the church of
baseball."

ANNIE SAVOY
Opening speech in "Bull Durham"

"Next to religion, baseball has furnished a
greater impact on American life than any
other institution."

HERBERT HOOVER

THE BEAUTIFUL GAME

"I love baseball, you know it doesn't have to
mean anything, it's just very beautiful to watch."
WOODY ALLEN

●

"It frequently escapes from the pattern of
sport and assumes the form of a virile
ballet.... The movement is natural and
unrehearsed and controlled only by the
unexpected flight of the ball."
JIMMY CANNON

●

"Any baseball is beautiful. No other small
package comes as close to the ideal in design
and utility. It is a perfect object for a man's
hand. Pick it up and it instantly suggests
its purpose. It is meant to be thrown
a considerable distance – thrown hard
and with precision."
ROGER ANGELL

THE PITCHER'S ART

"Pitching a game is really a memory test, like
playing a game of cards where you must
remember every card that has been played."

HOWARD EHMKE
Detroit Tigers pitcher 1916-1922

●

"The pitcher is the happiest with his arm idle.
He prefers to dawdle in the present, knowing
that as soon as he gets on the mound and
starts his windup, he delivers himself to the
uncertainty of the future."

GEORGE PLIMPTON
from "Out of My League"

●

"Pitching is the art of instilling fear."

SANDY KOUFAX
Brooklyn Dodgers pitcher 1955-1966

●

"It helps if the hitter thinks you're a little crazy."

NOLAN RYAN
Houston Astros pitcher 1980-1988

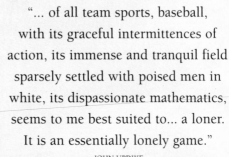

"... of all team sports, baseball,
with its graceful intermittences of
action, its immense and tranquil field
sparsely settled with poised men in
white, its dispassionate mathematics,
seems to me best suited to... a loner.
It is an essentially lonely game."

JOHN UPDIKE
from "Hub Fans Bid Kid Adieu" in "Assorted Prose"

FIELD OF ILLUSIONS

"Baseball fosters illusions. Baseball fosters hopes. Baseball inflates us. Baseball lies to us seductively and we know we're being seduced and we don't complain."

JOHN THORN

●

"There are surprisingly few real students of the game in baseball, partly because everybody, my 83-year-old mother included, thinks they learned all there was to know about it at puberty. Baseball is very beguiling that way."

ALVIN DARK
from "When in Doubt, Fire the Manager"

●

"Any time you think you have the game conquered, the game will turn around and punch you right in the nose."

MIKE SCHMIDT
Philadelphia Phillies third baseman 1972-1988

●

KIND OF DUMB

"If the mark of a grand passion is that you can love it even when it's kind of dumb, then baseball wins out by inches, one game at a time. Baseball is pre-eminently the talking man's game and who cares, or even notices, if the conversation is sometimes awesomely dull?"

WILFRID SHEED
from "Diamonds Are Forever" in "The New York Times Magazine"

●

"Baseball is the only field of endeavor where a man can succeed three times out of ten and be considered a good performer."

TED WILLIAMS
Boston Red Sox outfielder 1939-1942, 1946-1960

●

"The clock doesn't matter in baseball. Time stands still or moves backward. Theoretically, one game could go on forever. Some seem to."

HERB CAEN
Columnist, the "San Francisco Chronicle", 1979

"Baseball may be loved without statistics, but it cannot be understood without them. Statistics are what makes baseball a sport rather than a spectacle, what makes its past as worthy of our interest as well as its present."

JOHN THORN and PETE PALMER
from "The Hidden Game of Baseball"

●

"A baseball fan has the digestive apparatus of a billy goat. He can, and does, devour any set of diamond statistics with an insatiable appetite and then nuzzles hungrily for more."

ARTHUR DALEY
Sportswriter

●

"Statistics are to baseball what a flaky crust is to Mom's apple pie."

HARRY REASONER

●

AN UMP'S HEART

There once was an umpire whose vision
Was cause for abuse and derision.
He remarked in surprise,
"Why pick on my eyes?
It's my heart that dictates my decision."

OGDEN NASH
in the "Saturday Evening Post", 1966, and in "The Third Fireside Book of Baseball"
edited by Charles Einstein

●

"Umpire's heaven is a place where
he works third base every game. Home is
where the heartache is."

RON LUCIANO
American League umpire 1968-1980

●

"Gentlemen, he was out because I said
he was out."

BILL KLEM
National League umpire 1905-1941

●

LOSING IS SORT OF FUNNY...

"Losing streaks are funny.
If you lose at the beginning, you got off to a
bad start. If you lose in the middle of the
season, you're in a slump. If you lose at the
end, you're choking."

GENE MAUCH
Philadelphia Phillies manager 1960-1968

"If a tie is like kissing your sister, losing is like kissing your grandmother with her teeth out."

GEORGE BRETT

●

"I've heard of guys going 0 for 15 or 0 for 25, but I was 0 for July."

BOB ASPROMONTE

●

"We made too many wrong mistakes."

YOGI BERRA
His explanation for the Yankees losing the 1960 World Series to the Pittsburgh Pirates

●

"This losing streak is bad for the fans, no doubt, but look at it this way. We're making a lot of people happy in other cities."

TED TURNER

●

"We lost 13 straight one year. I decided if we got rained out, we'd have a victory party."

LEFTY GOMEZ
on managing in the minors

"For many, baseball cards are the last toy as well as the first possession. You fall in love with them as a child, then leave them behind at puberty. They link the blue-water, lazy-day joy of childhood summers with the pride of blossoming maturity."

THOMAS BOSWELL
in the "Washington Post", 1991

●

"... I couldn't go through a full summer's day without feverishly going through my card collection; letting my miserly hands run through the thousands of cards I kept in a box."

DANNY PEARY
from "How to Buy, Trade and Invest in Baseball Cards"

●

"I wanted to be a big league baseball player so I could see my picture on a bubblegum card."

AL FERRARA
Dodgers outfielder 1963-1968

●

MICKEY
MANTLE
N. Y. YANKEES   OF

WORLD SERIES!

"The World Series is American sport's annual ticket to a romantic yesterday, when we were all young and surely going to be in the big leagues someday."

RAY FITZGERALD
from "The Sporting News", 1981

●

"Many of us can no more remember our first World Series exposure than our first hot dog or first haircut. That is because it is an experience woven and rewoven into so much of our existence."

EDWIN POPE
from "Mark Twain's World Series"

●

"No presidential campaign can seriously begin until after the World Series."

JOHN F. KENNEDY
35th President of the United States

●

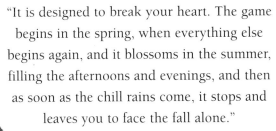

"It is designed to break your heart. The game begins in the spring, when everything else begins again, and it blossoms in the summer, filling the afternoons and evenings, and then as soon as the chill rains come, it stops and leaves you to face the fall alone."

A. BARTLETT GIAMATTI

"People ask me what I do in winter when there's no baseball. I'll tell you what I do, I stare out the window and wait for spring."

ROGERS HORNSBY
St. Louis Cardinals player and manager 1915-1926

LINKING THE GENERATIONS

"The history of other sports seems to begin
anew with each generation, but
baseball, that wondrous myth
of twentieth century
America, gets passed on
like an inheritance."

STANLEY COHEN
from "The Man in the Crowd", 1981

●

"... I feel an invisible bond among
our three generations, an anchor of loyalty
linking my sons to the grandfather whose
face they have never seen but whose
person they have come to know
through this most timeless of all sports."

DORIS KEARNS GOODWIN
from "From Father, With Love" in the "Boston Globe", October 6, 1986

"Baseball's time is seamless and invisible, a bubble within which players move at exactly the same pace and rhythms as all their predecessors.... Since baseball time is measured only in outs, all you have to do is succeed utterly; keep hitting, keep the rally alive, and you have defeated time. You remain forever young."

ROGER ANGELL

A LEGACY

"All I want out of life is that when I walk down the street folks will say, 'There goes the greatest hitter that ever lived.'"

TED WILLIAMS
Boston Red Sox outfielder 1939-1942, 1946-1960

●

"Nothing flatters me more than to have it assumed that I could write prose – unless it be to have it assumed that I once pitched a baseball with distinction."

ROBERT FROST

●

"... I think there are only three things that America will be known for 2,000 years from now when they study this civilization: the Constitution, jazz music, and baseball. They're the three most beautifully designed things this culture has ever produced."

GERALD EARLY